RED ROCK
EDEN

The Story of Fruita

One of Mormon Country's Most Isolated Settlements

GEORGE E. DAVIDSON

Capitol Reef Natural History Association
Capitol Reef National Park

© 1986 by Capitol Reef Natural History Association
Edited and reprinted 2002.

ISBN 1-887517-03-0

Capitol Reef Natural History Association
Capitol Reef National Park
Torrey, Utah 84775

Design and composition by Sandy Bell, Springdale, Utah
Cartography by David Fuller, DLF Group, Santa Barbara, California
Printing by Lorraine Press, Salt Lake City, Utah

Special thanks are due Cora Oyler Smith, Lila Behunin Ham, Marjorie
Cook Krantz, G. Neldon Adams and the Utah State Historical Society
for the use of their photographs.

COVER: Nels Johnson, wife May
and son William. Photograph taken
in Junction in the late 1800s.

BACK COVER: Harold Edward
Nixon, grandson of Calvin David
Pendleton, photographed in Fruita
about 1911.

PAGE 1: The young daughters of
Fruita settler M. V. Oyler photographed about 1912.

*This book is dedicated to
Evangeline Ostberg Tappan Godby,
the Wayne County historian whose depth of feeling
for those long gone inspired its writing.*

*The second printing of this book
is dedicated to the author, George E. Davidson.
His love for the history of this area and its people
inspired him to record their stories
for future generations.*

Fruita used to be one of our favorite places—a sudden, intensely green little valley among the cliffs of the Waterpocket Fold, opulent with cherries, peaches, and apples in season, inhabited by a few families who were about equally good Mormons and good frontiersmen and good farmers.

Contents

A different kind of frontier history...

I remember when a businessman visiting Capitol Reef National Park shared with me his dream for the creation of a "frontier village" near here. I listened—with all the deadpan I could muster—to his enthusiastic conjuring of a vision of swinging door saloon, town marshal's office, bank, livery stable, and staged "shoot-outs" between outlaws and lawmen. I hope my response to that scheme was enough to park it permanently on the isle of ought-to-be-lost ideas.

The rootin', tootin', violence of old Tombstone, range wars, roaring mining camps, surrounded wagon trains, and galloping cavalry was rarely woven into the fabric of the history of south-central Utah. Here, very close to the end of America's frontier period, droplets of the Euro-American floodtide trickled into slickrock niches near the Colorado Plateau's Fremont River, named for John Charles Fremont. The usual human flotsam of America's frontier drifted here, too—rustlers, thieves, "sharpers"—but in a ratio to the God-fearing population that seems to have been fairly small. Most of these, except for Butch Cassidy's Wild Bunch, are totally forgotten, even in local histories.

In large measure, the frontier history of Utah is the history of the Latter-day Saints (Mormons). It was no different along the lower Fremont River in the 1880s, although the influence of the Salt Lake City-based Mormon Church and her leadership was often diluted by the harsh isolation. Just how isolated? Well, as late as 1961, when the interstate highway system was well on its way to linking together mainstream America with high-tech, asphalt ribbons, it took the better part of a day to creep the thirty-five miles from Fruita to Hanksville over a meandering, unpaved track known as the Blue Dugway.

Any locale at all on the lower Fremont River was very, very difficult to get to or from—literally the end of the earth in the contiguous forty-eight states.

More than a century ago, a half-dozen brave, new settlements were sited along the lower Fremont between its exit from the deep gorges of Miners Mountain and its confluence with the Muddy River. Most are now forgotten—Aldridge, Clifton, Giles, Elephant—but others are still peopled, like Hanksville and Caineville. The little community called Fruita—never more than ten families—found itself deep inside Capitol Reef National Monument after a Presidential proclamation in 1937. Although its new relationship with the National Park Service would become a tolling bell for Fruita as a living relic of the frontier, it insured, paradoxically, that it would be remembered. I think some of the old settlers would be tickled to know that today their tale is fascinating to many park visitors from all over the world.

In 1980, as a newly arrived ranger charged with sharing Capitol Reef National Park's resources with vacationing visitors, I became interested in its little-told human history. Except for the helpful foundation work done by Mr. Gerald Hoddenbach, a former park scientist with a fascination for history, we held little in our park files. I gathered material from libraries, privately held journals, and oral history interviews with elderly residents who had experienced the isolated life of the lower Fremont River communities early in the century. This booklet owes a lot to their candor and helpfulness.

At this writing, only the boldest threads of the story of Fruita and the lower Fremont River homesteaders have come to light and accounts are full of contradiction. Notwithstanding, interest in this gentle green oasis, nestled in one of America's newest national parks, demands some kind of publication now, even "a wine before its time." The chapter titles are derived from a majestic and stirring Mormon hymn.

George E. Davidson
Chief, Interpretation and Information Services
Capitol Reef National Park
December 1985

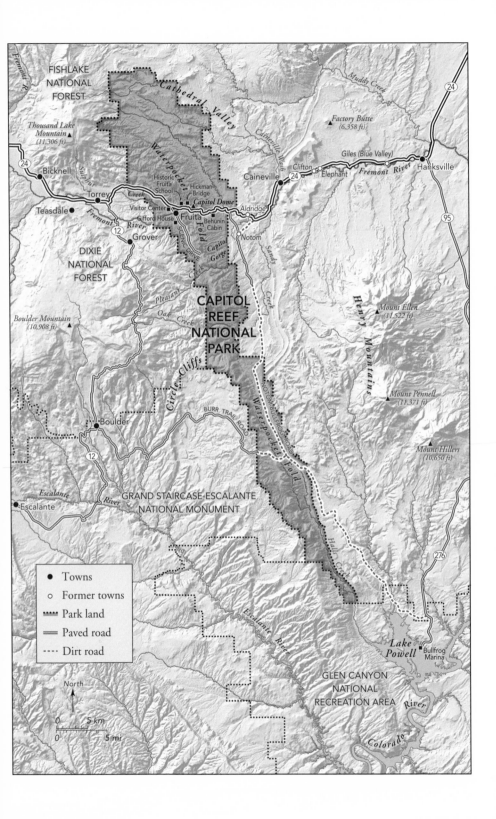

FISHLAKE
NATIONAL
FOREST

*Thousand Lake
Mountain*
(11,306 ft)

Bicknell

Torrey

Teasdale

Grover

DIXIE
NATIONAL
FOREST

*Boulder Mountain
(10,908 ft)*

Boulder

*Escalante
River*

Escalante

GRAND STAIRCASE-ESCALANTE
NATIONAL MONUMENT

Cathedral Valley

Muddy Creek

*Factory Butte
(6,358 ft)*

Giles (Blue Valley)

Caineville

Clifton
Elephant

Fremont River

Hanksville

Historic
Fruita
School

Hickman
Bridge

Capitol Dome

Visitor Center

Gifford House Fruita

Behunin
Cabin

Aldridge

Notom

*Capitol
Gorge*

CAPITOL
REEF
NATIONAL
PARK

Henry Mountains

*Mount Ellen
(11,522 ft)*

*Mount Pennell
(11,371 ft)*

*Mount Hillers
(10,650 ft)*

Pleasant

Oak Creek

Circle Cliffs

BURR TRAIL ROAD

Waterpocket Fold

Halls Creek

Lake
Powell

Bullfrog
Marina

GLEN CANYON
NATIONAL
RECREATION
AREA

Colorado River

- Towns
○ Former towns
···· Park land
— Paved road
--- Dirt road

North

0 ___ 5 km
0 ___ 5 mi

Come, come ye Saints

The date of a human's first visit to the Waterpocket Fold country cannot be told. Hunter-gatherer nomads may have visited the area often in the millennia before the first evidences of occupation were left by aboriginal agriculturalists.

The Fremont Culture began occupying Utah about the same time as the western Roman Empire was being totally demolished. Scholars divide the culture into five groups; it was the San Rafael group of the Fremont Culture that occupied niches in and around the Waterpocket Fold and shared a cultural boundary with the better-known, pueblo-building Anasazi. The Fremont Culture people left their long-occupied sites during a complex and imperfectly understood population upheaval in the thirteenth century. Never great builders, their most intriguing legacy to modern man is a pervasive and elaborate rock art.

When white men first began rambling around the lands near the Waterpocket Fold after the Civil War, they encountered nomadic Indians—mostly Utes and Paiutes. Some encounters were violent, especially with the Utes, but after the Blackhawk War the Indians were no longer a real barrier to exploration and settlement of the lands near the fold.

As the last territory to be explored in the contiguous forty-eight states, the Waterpocket Fold country was not charted by credible scientists until Professor Almon H. Thompson's

OPPOSITE: Fremont petroglyphs found along the Fremont River in Fruita.

The men then worked their way down the canyon into oxen country. When they reached the flat land at a small lake or pond called Red Lake, not far from Thousand Lake Mountain, they halted. General Snow and Colonel Ivie went up a black rocky ridge to get a view of the surrounding country.

As they neared the top, Colonel Ivie saw a ramrod wiggling behind a bush only a few yards away and exclaimed, "There they are." His shout was followed by a volley from ambush, one bullet hitting and seriously wounding General Snow in the shoulder.

The men retreated to their company and a battle ensued. Firing from ambush on top of the hill, the Indians overshot their mark, most of their bullets whizzing over the heads of the soldiers into the water below. None of the men were killed, but two were wounded—Orson Taylor of Richfield and George Franken of Mt. Pleasant.

Officers then ordered a short retreat in order to get a flanking movement of the savages. After the men had fallen back, they noticed one of their pack animals had been left behind. Ezra Shoemaker of Manti and another man went back through a shower of bullets from the enemy and recovered the animal with its pack. The fighting continued until night, several Indians being killed during the fray.

—as recorded by Anne Snow in *Rainbow Views*, courtesy of the Daughters of the Utah Pioneers.

reconnoitering party from Kanab entered the region in 1872. Young Frederick Dellenbaugh, an assistant map maker on the Thompson expedition, was very uneasy when they encountered a small band of Utes while descending from Boulder Mountain into the fold country. The Indians seemed frightened and one of the two squaws they first stumbled upon raised a knife at Dellenbaugh and rushed toward him. He could have killed her with his Winchester but kept his head and just laughed at her, which stopped the attack cold. It could have turned into a bloodbath. Later, they discovered that the Ute band of some eight men with their families was probably the same group that had attacked one of the Sevier County settlements and killed a child. The unusual fear and shyness displayed by the band then seemed clear to Dellenbaugh. A year earlier, brave, lonely travelers (probably miners) had begun carving their names into the soft sandstone walls of Capitol Gorge, initiating a pioneer register.

Explorers and a few bold miners aside, the history of white settlement of south-central Utah is Mormon history. In the years between Brigham Young's first look at the valley of the Great Salt Lake in 1847 and the Civil War, Mormon pioneers flowed southward to St. George, Utah, along that long, but fairly narrow, corridor of arable land between the Great Basin to the West and the Colorado Plateau on the east.

The creation of isolated pockets of non-Mormons elsewhere in Zion, mostly mining communities, became a matter of considerable concern to the Church. Apparently, the leadership encouraged Mormon occupation of every nook and cranny of the Utah territory to forestall too many gentile inroads. Except when the Church actually directed individuals to move and resettle in a remote area (a mission), this pressure was informal. But given the hard-charging frontiersman spirit of the Utah Mormons and the desire to make a home in the wilderness, it is often difficult to determine the motives of any given pioneer tackling the hardships of moving on.

In the late 1870s and early 1880s, pioneers exploded from the confines of the St. George–Salt Lake corridor and into the forbidding Colorado Plateau country to the east. In south-central Utah, the signal event for the explosion was the moving of a large herd of horses and cattle from the corridor town of Richfield eastward to a lush valley in the high plateaus known as Rabbit Valley, about thirty miles west of the Waterpocket Fold.

Mormon scout Albert K. Thurber had been directed by Brigham Young to explore the lands just west of the Waterpocket Fold for their settlement potential. Thurber helped care for that Richfield cattle herd and, in 1874, built several cabins in a grassy area now called Bicknell Bottoms. By the end of the decade, the rapid influx of settlers had laid the blueprint for western Wayne County and for the little communities that would eventually become Fremont, Loa, Lyman, Bicknell, Teasdale, Grover, and Torrey.

Albert K. Thurber not only explored and initiated Mormon settlement of Wayne County, but had been instrumental in negotiating a peace with local Utes that made such settlement feasible.

Nels Johnson, perhaps the Waterpocket Fold's first true settler.

Most of the early pioneers were sheepmen and cattlemen; the high, dry, short-season plateau climate was not conducive to agriculture. Although farming has improved with more sophisticated irrigation systems and methods, Wayne County is still cattle and sheep country, even though the sheep business has declined over the last few decades.

In 1878, the ominously broken, unpopulated red rock country to the east of Rabbit Valley beckoned insistently. To be sure, like Bryce Canyon, most of it was a "bad place to lose a cow," but the narrow-valley flood plains of its year-round watercourses held some promise for farmers.

Today, from the broad shoulders of Boulder Mountain, the tourist's colorful view across the jumbled Waterpocket Fold east to the Henry Mountains is incomparable. This same view, however, must have been a little ominous for a restless pioneer considering gambling his family's welfare (even their lives) on *living* there.

All evidence points to Franklin D. Young as the first (about 1878) to risk making a livelihood deep in the slickrock wilderness. Young's father, Franklin W. Young, was an active, civic-minded Mormon well-known in the older Rabbit Valley settlements but we still know little about his namesake son.[1] Apparently, Franklin D. Young never completed establishing a homestead at the junction of Sulphur Creek and the Fremont River, the future site of Fruita. History has labeled him a "squatter."

Soon after Young gave up, Nels Johnson moved to the junction in 1880 and staked his homestead. He may have been the first bona fide settler in the Waterpocket Fold country. Others followed quickly, and within three years settlements had tenuous footholds along the Fremont River all the way to the confluence of that watercourse with the Muddy River. But Fruita was the first.

Only twenty years after the battle near Red Lake the proud, combative Utes had been pacified. In 1888, a *Deseret News* writer described Poganeab, their once-proud leader, near Fish Lake:

At this lake I got an introduction to a noted character in these parts, the Chief or Fish-Captain, the hereditary owner of the lake, Poggy. I have seen Indians, but the look of this one left an impression upon my mind not soon to be forgotten. . . . There he sits upon a pony, void of muscle, clothed in rags of various kinds with battered kettles suspended to the saddle tree, his grizzled hair cropped off, toothless, wrinkled and his horse stooping both ways from where he sat. If a nickel is handed to him, he smiles in ghastly gratitude and chattering passes on. Alas poor Poggy. But a few more snows and he will be gathered to the happy hunting grounds, rolled away in his tattered blanket, his wickieup burned. His watery domain will be usurped, for the citizens of this valley have already expended over six hundred dollars putting in a dam and an outlet to Fish Lake.

1   Franklin W. Young coined the sobriquet "Eden of Wayne County" for Fruita in an 1898 *Deseret News* article.

No toil nor labor fear

We have some idea of what Fruita looked like when pioneers arrived at the confluence of the Fremont with Sulphur Creek. According to cattleman Howard Blackburn, who passed through the unsettled area as a boy, the valley was matted with a tangled growth of squawbush. The thick soil of the valley floor was strewn with black, volcanic boulders washed down from the high country by raging glacial melt-waters of the last Ice Age.

Clearing the land must have been difficult, but perhaps not as backbreaking as the chore facing earlier-day pioneers in the eastern hardwood forests. Squawbush is shallow rooted and fairly easy to tear out and burn. The black rocks may not have been much of a problem, either. Today, there are no especially big rock piles anywhere in Fruita; the stones comprising the cattle-restraining drift fences on the side of Johnson Mesa were probably gathered from that immediate locale. Tradition records that remains of ancient irrigation ditches of the Fremont Culture were evident everywhere but these were soon lost to the plowshare.

OPPOSITE: Julia Ellen Cook, 15, and Isaac Martin Behunin, 24, held their wedding reception in the Fruita schoolhouse in 1904. Both were the children of early Fruita settlers; Julia's parents were Joseph Ridley Cook and Mary Ann Taylor Cook. Isaac was a son of Elijah Cutler Behunin and Tabitha Jane Earl Behunin. Isaac and Julia Behunin began their family early. Here, in 1905, they pose with first-born daughter Angela. They had twelve more children.

Today, the historic area of Fruita comprises three hundred acres, more or less—not much space for agriculture, western-style. But one element favored the land here more than the sprawling high valleys to the west—abundant and easily accessible water. Then too, this junction of two perennial waterflows was 2,000 feet lower than Rabbit Valley and had a longer growing season. Settlers found that the canyon walls reflected heat to the good soil below. Smallish Fruita may not have been well suited for the grain economy of the high valleys, but it was ideal for one product in great demand on the frontier—fresh fruit.

Apparently, Nels Johnson himself planted the first orchards soon after constructing a small cabin about two hundred feet from the Fremont River and immediately to the west of what is now the Scenic Drive of Capitol Reef National Park. Pioneers planted varieties of apples that have almost disappeared or are completely gone from today's Fruita apple orchards—apples like the Jonathan, Rome Beauty, Ben Davis, Red Astrachan, Twenty-ounce Pippin and Yellow Transparent. Other fruits of those early orchards are still popular: Morpark apricot, Elberta peach, Bartlett pear, Fellenburg plum and that great favorite of the Mormon pioneers, the Potawatomi plum. Johnson also planted nut trees—English walnut, black walnut, and almond. Within a decade, grape arbors were everywhere and later became the basis of a thriving—but illegal—local industry. The appearance of the little valley changed rapidly in a few short years.

Farmer Nels Johnson was joined eventually by pioneers just as land hungry and ambitious as himself. His

The road through Capitol Wash (now called Capitol Gorge) was a rough, hard-to-keep-clear passage to the settlements downriver from Fruita and remained the only motor road through the Waterpocket Fold until 1962. This photograph was taken about 1919 and shows a Ford Model T with two freight wagons.

Elijah Cutler Behunin was a dynamic frontiersman and born leader. Like so many of his frontier contemporaries, he moved his large family often. During the 1890s, he resided in Junction (Fruita) where he helped build the schoolhouse and became Junction's first presiding elder for the Mormon Church. The photograph was taken in Junction about 1896 and shows Behunin with wife Tabitha Jane and eleven of their thirteen children.

brother, John, built a house directly across the Fremont River from Nels. The Behunins, Sorensons, Holts, and Pierces became neighbors. Other names briefly associated with Junction (the town was later renamed Fruita) during this early period include Gilbert Adams, Cynthia Rogers, Charles Mulford, and Matthew W. Mansfield. History does not record whether or not Nels Johnson was glad for the company; it does not record much at all about him or his family. He was known as a hard worker and very thrifty; a legend persisted for years that he buried his money somewhere in Fruita, which was never found after he fell into the Fremont River and drowned in 1902. The Bishop of Torrey officiated at graveside services in Teasdale (it appears no one was ever buried in Fruita) and noted in his journal that "...I was one of the speakers—had a large crowd—his folks took it very hard." [1]

The unfortunate Nels Johnson seems to have been one of only a few residents to have expired in Fruita. Young Clara Oyler was one of two girls stricken with typhoid fever about 1918; she died while little Thelma

1   "The Journal of John Riley Stewart" in the archives of The Church of Jesus Christ of Latter-day Saints, Salt Lake City. Used with permission.

19

The Holt Homesteaders

Leo and Rena (Anna Laurina) Holt were some of the earliest settlers to file for a homestead in Fruita.

Their first home in Fruita was a boarded-up tent and it was there, in 1895, that their first child was born. Little Iva May, however, died of a scorpion sting at age three months.

Leo Holt was an accomplished stonemason, as well as carpenter, and introduced the use of adobe for buildings made from the local soils. He helped build the school in 1896.

Rena Holt was very active in church work and served many years as president of the Mormon Church's women's organization in Fruita (The Relief Society). She was well known as a competent midwife and delivered at least fifty-five babies, most without the oversight of a physician. She usually stayed with mother and newborn child for at least ten days following delivery and her total fee was ten dollars, often settled with bartered farm produce instead of cash.

The Holt House, built about 1898, no longer exists in one sense; it has been so altered and added to since the 1920s that Leo and Rena Holt would not recognize it. However, the black rock wall that once fronted a quiet country lane (now Utah 24) is still there, as well as a clay-roofed root cellar, built by Leo Holt after the turn of the century.

Between 1919 and 1940, the home was owned first by Clarence Mulford and then by Alma Chesnut. After 1940, the home was owned by the National Park Service and served as the residence for the park's first superintendent—Charles Kelly.

—based, in part, on the recollections of Irene Holt Busenbark.

Pendleton survived. Elsewhere along the Fremont, diphtheria and influenza took a tragic toll, as well as typhoid. Emergency medical care was often more than eighty hard miles away and treatment was given by family and neighbors instead. Once a veterinarian happened to be passing through Blue Valley and assisted in amputating the gangrenous leg of Bishop Henry Giles, who did not survive the cutting made without an anesthetic.

After Fruita, or "Junction" as it was first known, the wayfarer would find Aldridge, Caineville, Elephant, Blue Valley, Clifton, and finally, Hanksville (or Graves Valley). Early in the 1880s, settlers had to use the narrow Fremont River Valley to haul a wagon east of Fruita and through the Waterpocket Fold. This route necessitated dozens of river fordings. In 1883, however, a group of pioneers, led by Elijah Cutler Behunin, cleared a narrow wagon road through Capitol Gorge, long favored as a trail through the fold by local Indians. This route became vital not only for the provisioning of downriver settlements, but to sheep and cattlemen who soon settled into a pattern of wintering huge herds on the lands northeast and southeast of the Fremont River Valley and returning them to the high country near Loa in the summer. Eventually, a wagon road was built all the way to Hanksville, mostly along the river banks, and called the Blue Dugway for the pale blue clays it traversed. The road through the gorge remained open until 1962, when Highway 24 was rerouted through the Fremont River Canyon.

The Blue Dugway became Fruita's link to the rest of the human race and a source of cash income. Over it passed miners, sheepshearers, Mormon Church officials, settlers en route, cattle with attendants, lawmen, outlaws, Indians, even gypsies by one account, and individual herds of sheep numbering in the thousands. By most accounts, fresh and dried fruits, vegetables, wine, and moonshine were always ready for purchase or barter in Fruita.

Cattlemen and sheepherders first used open areas in Fruita for overnight camping, but a desire for a roof over their heads soon brought about the construction of a long building with fireplaces. It was simply called the camp house and it stood near the still-standing Jorgenson–Gifford Barn. The builder and first innkeeper

The Blue Dugway was a starkly picturesque, lonely and slow wagon road from Fruita to Hanksville from the 1880s until 1962. One wagoneer reported confronting the cloven-hooved devil himself at a bend in the road but that he was able to save himself only by waving a copy of the *Book of Mormon* at Satan's leering visage.

A settler of Blue Valley remembered the ravages of disease suffered by the Fremont River pioneers:

Saint Vitus Dance was a very prevalent disease among the children of our little community and the people believed they were possessed of the Devil, as they would do and say many peculiar things while under the influence of these attacks. Maybe the Devil did have something to do with it and they were more susceptible under their weakened condition but, as I assess it today, in my opinion it was lack of proper nourishment. We had the same food as everyone else but our family was never afflicted and we saw much suffering among our neighbors and several unexplainable deaths. Two of our finest young women caught little colds and were found dead in their beds the next morning for no explainable reason. Then smallpox hit our town. Henry Giles contracted it while in Emery County after supplies. When he got home the whole family was stricken and helpless within a week. A town meeting was called, everyone was scared pink as smallpox was a killer in those days. The Giles family had to have help as they were all down and lived across the river away from the town. Father volunteered to go and take care of them. He cooked, washed and saw them through. Mother and I would ride down to the river and visit with father by yelling across.

—from the reminiscences of James William Nielson, Blue Valley pioneer.

The late nineteenth century pioneers who homesteaded along the lower Fremont River called it the Dirty Devil and this practice has confused those familiar with modern nomenclature of south-central Utah's watercourses. During the late nineteenth and early twentieth centuries, the river seemed more inclined to meander during heavy floods and was very destructive to crops and elaborate ditch irrigation systems, especially in settlements like Caineville and Blue Valley.

This modern photograph was taken near Blue Valley, abandoned before World War I, now marked only by a few ruined structures and a sad little graveyard that attests to the ravages of typhoid fever, smallpox and other diseases. Blue Valley was a challenge to which not even rawhide-tough Mormon pioneers were equal.

2 Oral history transcript in the archives of the Church of Jesus Christ of Latter-day Saints, Salt Lake City. Used with permission.

of the camp house is unknown; the first name associated with its management is Calvin Pendleton. As a young Caineville resident, Evangeline Ostberg Tappan Godby remembered another small hotel. She stayed there in Fruita when her family visited Uncle Joe and Aunt Mary Ann Cook about 1908. Her father, Alfred Ostberg, was a leading citizen of Caineville.

Twenty years after the first settlers arrived, the small family orchards of Fruita were in production. A trip to Fruita during the harvest season became a regular outing for many families living on the colder plateaus to the west. Sarah Williams Stringham, who was born in Teasdale, recalled:

In the summertime we often went to Fruita, about twenty miles away, for peaches and grapes. Teasdale was higher and colder than Fruita and we couldn't grow these fruits. We would go in the afternoon, camp overnight, pick the fruit in the morning and come home again. Sometimes three or four cousins would go and stay about two weeks. They would pick, cut and dry fruit for the owner of the orchard. As pay for this work the owner would give them as much fresh fruit as they had picked and dried for him. [2]

The last two decades of the nineteenth century proved that the settlers of Fruita had unknowingly made a wise choice in locating in the valley where they did. The water that they had first worried about became a problem in the valley below Fruita, not because of a shortage thereof, but because of a dangerous overabundance.

Around the turn of the century, the Fremont River was less confined to a stable course and it was more inclined to meander during flooding. Paiute nomads near Caineville had warned pioneers there of the danger, but no one took them seriously. From 1890 through the early twentieth century, flooding of massive proportions devastated the settlements downriver from Fruita and eventually made ghost towns of several. But, because Fruita's orchards and fields stood a little higher along a more deeply incised watercourse, it was usually spared heavy damage. Mrs. Evangeline Godby has vivid recollections of the flood of 1909, which mostly deal with Caineville, her childhood home. Fruita is mentioned, however:

> . . . the flood came so heavy through Fruita that it carried trees, still full of apples, all the way to Caineville. The fruit trees were just tumbling over and over in the mud. There were fat pigs still swimming in it when they got to Caineville.[3]

Just what did such floods do to life-sustaining fields and orchards in Caineville? Mrs. Godby wrote eloquently about it in the *Deseret News:*

> . . . they saw whole fields disappear in the jaws of the flood. Great chunks of land split from the solid earth, seemed to rise, sway and explode with a bang, sucked down in the red foam, boiling and dying like a living thing.
>
> The whole valley was filled with the boom, as from cannons; the roar of the water and the stench of a dying world.[4]

Although Fruita residents saw many a flood, they never saw anything like that, nor the horrendous destruction it caused in communities downriver.

The flooding of the Fremont River in Fruita was never the disaster it was further downriver, but it was something to remember, nevertheless. This photograph depicts a major flood on September 3, 1945, when much of the north valley floor of Fruita was under water. The villain in that disaster was Sulphur Creek, however, not the Fremont.

In 1985, the Fremont River went on a rampage and destroyed the Scenic Drive bridge and a park building. A similar flood in 1937 had torn away an earlier bridge and threatened the home of Fruita resident Dewey Gifford.

3   Interview with Mrs. Evangeline Ostberg Tappan Godby, September 2, 1981.

4   Article in *Deseret News*, July 1981.

Though hard to you the journey may appear

Stories abound about Butch Cassidy's Wild Bunch traveling the Blue Dugway from their Robbers' Roost hideout (near Hanksville) to Loa and back but no Fruita stories about them have been found except that they had a hideout near Grand Wash. The place that some believe was once such a Wild Bunch hideout may have been instead a refuge for Mormon polygamists pursued doggedly by federal lawmen in the 1880s. The Cassidy legend in Wayne County is filled with contradictions, although we know that Deputy U.S. Marshal Joe Bush did arrest two Robbers' Roost denizens. "Blue John" and "Silver Tip" were tried in Loa at the turn of the century; the records are still on file at the courthouse.

The late 1880s were years of almost unbearable stress for the Utah Territory Mormons and their Church. A forty-year-old feud with the federal government was reaching another explosive point. New federal laws had made polygamy a felony and a large force of deputy U.S. marshals was scouring the territory for violators to be brought before non-Mormon juries. Worse yet for the Mormons, the corporate assets of their Church had been seized and were being held hostage. The federal government pressure intensified until

Ephraim K. Hanks, shown here as a younger man, was described as "a middle-sized, light-haired, good-looking man, with regular features, a pleasant and humorous countenance, and the manly manner of his early sailor's life touched with the rough cordiality of the mountaineer (while) ... frank as a bear-hunter." Frontier Utah saw few tougher or more resolute men than Hanks.

Many Mormon women who were plural wives admitted that they would never have accepted it had it not been for the requirements of their religion. But there was another side to the coin:

The status advantages of being a plural wife have seldom been seriously considered. Non-Mormon critics of polygamy have almost invariably assumed that since they would have felt degraded under plural marriage, plural wives must also have felt degraded. Plausible though this might seem, little internal Mormon evidence supports such a view. Life certainly did hold special trials for plural wives, but at least until the 1880s, being a plural wife brought higher status through association with the most influential men and through a sense of serving as a religious and social model for others. First wives such as Jane Richards who married under monogamous expectations often had considerable difficulty in adjusting, but many plural wives had other reactions. In some cases, first wives actively encouraged a reluctant husband to take a plural wife so that they could both reach the highest state of exaltation in the afterlife or for other more pragmatic economic or personal considerations. Viewed as an honorable and desirable practice, plural marriage could give women a sense of pride and significance within the Mormon Community.

—from "Polygamy and the Frontier: Mormon Women in Early Utah" by Lawrence Foster in the Utah Historical Quarterly, Summer, 1982.

1890 when the Mormon Church president declared in a manifesto that "the Mormon people will no longer practice polygamy." With that, the federal campaign against the Utah Mormons ended abruptly, and within six years Utah was admitted to the Union.

Fugitive polygamists sought refuge in the tiny settlements lying in the shadow of the Waterpocket Fold, although only a small proportion of the earliest adult male Fruita settlers—if any—appear to have been violators of anti-polygamy statutes. Hanksville seems to have sheltered more polygamists than any other Fremont River settlement.

According to local tradition, the almost-invisible canyon to the east and high above the present Fruita campground earned its name from early settlers using it as a polygamist hiding place in the 1880s. This origin for the name Cohab Canyon has yet to be confirmed, however. What is confusing about this colorful handle is that "cohab" (cohabitationist) was an abusive slur used by non-Mormons to describe what the Mormons considered

ABOVE: Prisoners at the U.S. Penitentiary in Salt Lake City.

BELOW: Looking down upon the buildings of the Penitentiary.

The dilapidated U.S. Penitentiary at Salt Lake City could not accommodate the sudden influx of convicted polygamists:

At the peak of overpopulation in 1888, officials built three bunk-houses of two-by-sixes laid flat and spiked together for walls, floor, and ceiling. These provided an excellent breeding ground for bedbugs, a common Salt Lake pest in the best of households. Three-tier-high bunks, sleeping two in each, surrounded a small heating stove and an impossibly tiny center lounging area. Partitioned off in one corner was a wooden box and water barrel cut in two, called the "dunnigan," which did duty for the men during the night. A few barred windows and ventilating shafts in the roof relieved the stuffiness.

Other special residences within the yard were a hospital, solitary confinement facility, insane asylum cages, and two solitary "sweat boxes" used for extreme punishment.

The common bond of brotherhood in the church and common sacrifice brought these men together in their trials. To a man they believed that their constitutional rights were being infringed upon. Even some non-Mormons acquainted with the circumstances and integrity of the accused did not look upon this across-the-board incarceration of the Mormons as containing any element of crime or moral disgrace. One venerable pioneer who was sentenced for three months, plus the usual fine and costs, said "our incarceration was in fact an imprisonment for conscience sake, that being the position in which the law found us." Most of the men thought it ridiculous to be put in prison for what they referred to as living with their wives and taking care of their children.

—from "Life Behind Bars: Mormon Cohabs of the 1880s" by Melvin L. Bashmore in the *Utah Historical Quarterly*, Winter, 1979.

to be the divinely ordained institution of plural marriage. It is hard to imagine local Mormons using the word. Living old timers recall only one polygamist who actually resided in Fruita—Calvin Pendleton—but that was after the turn of the century. Some say the squatter Young was a polygamist but that is unconfirmed. The earliest days remain obscure.

Federal marshals came through Fruita over the dugway. Instead of continuing through Capitol Gorge to the downriver settlements, however, they often diverted their attentions to Floral Ranch—a few miles south of the west side of the gorge. It is not easy to tell the story of Fruita without at least sidelighting Floral Ranch, for here resided one of the most interesting players in the drama of Waterpocket Fold settlement—Ephraim K. Hanks.

"Eph" Hanks settled along a remote area of Pleasant Creek in 1882. He had been a frontier mail carrier, a scout for Mormon wagon trains moving into the valley of the Great Salt Lake thirty years earlier, and had served as a soldier in the Mormon Battalion. Hanks was thought by some to have been a bodyguard for the oft-threatened Brigham Young and was—it was said—no man to be toyed with. He had been a polygamist himself, but according to his family biographer had divorced all his wives and remarried the youngest, Thisbee, before moving to the fold country. Hanks and his family worked hard and, in a few short years, a house and farm outbuildings had been built and irrigation had made his desert homestead at Floral Ranch bloom.

The aging scout also operated an underground railroad at Floral Ranch for fugitive polygamists, much like some midwesterners and easterners of pre-Civil War America had sheltered, protected, and provided a "railroad" to freedom for thousands of fugitive black slaves. Many a Wayne County polygamist with an arrest warrant outstanding found shelter with Eph Hanks. When deputy U.S. marshals came into the county, sympathetic Mormons would get word to Hanks. Sometimes his son, Walter B. Hanks, would make a dangerous, short-cut ride on horseback down Pleasant Creek from Loa to arrive at the ranch before the slow-moving marshals. According to his biographer, Hanks was never caught at his game.

When the marshals arrived, there was never a fugitive to be found; they were well hidden in the back country. Hanks was much respected by his neighbors and was eventually made a patriarch of the Mormon Church, a high honor. He died of "congestion of the brain" in 1896.

As the decade of the 1880s ended, so did the arrest and prosecution of Mormon polygamists, even though the hated Edmunds Laws against polygamy were still on the books. In the valley of the Fremont, 1890 brought a respite from lawmen intruders and the peace of mind necessary to make real communities of the still-primitive settlements. It was almost a signal year, an end of the beginning for the Saints along the Fremont.

Gird up your loins, fresh courage take

For historian Frederick Jackson Turner, the year 1890 marked the closing of the American frontier. His "Turner thesis" conceptualized America's turning abroad to adventures in Cuba and the Philippines as the redirection of an exuberant, expansionist spirit once swallowed up by the unsettled vastness of the American West.

For the Saints at Fruita, the year of the frontier's closing meant that they had a secure foothold on the banks of the Fremont but nothing like a civilized community—no school, no church-meeting house, no post office. Since survival was assured by 1890, it was time to attend to a few amenities of civilization. That year, the first attempts at public education were made when twelve-year-old Nettie Behunin began teaching local children. It is only conjecture, but this instruction may have been related to the Mormon Church's primary program of religious instruction.

The first community-building project was the construction of a school. It is not clear who initiated the project but either Amasa Pierce or road builder Elijah Cutler Behunin contributed a small plot of land just below the soaring red cliffs of the escarpment. Pierce was a man of considerable influence and, after the turn of the century, he was

The Fruita schoolhouse was restored by the National Park Service in 1966 and is listed on the National Register of Historic Places. This 1937 photograph was taken just three years before the building was closed and Fruita children bussed up the valley. If you look closely, you can see outhouses in the background.

presiding elder in Fruita for the Mormon Church. In the
almost-total absence of any civil authority, Pierce's guid-
ance was a reality to be reckoned with. Regardless of
whomever actually donated the small plot of land for the
school, Pierce, Behunin, and Leo Holt seem to have been
the planners and primary builders.

The little one-room structure was completed in 1896.
It was made of hewn logs, had a flat roof covered with
bentonite clay, which resists penetration by water (a
peaked, shingled roof was added about 1914). Its interior
was not finished (plastering was added in 1935) but the
logs were well chinked and the wood stove was more than
enough to keep it cozy in winter. For some reason,
county-sanctioned instruction did not begin in the
schoolhouse until 1900. At that time, twenty-two-year-old
Nettie Behunin Noyes taught the first official classes and
the school remained open until 1941, when the Fruita
children were bussed to consolidated schools, and the
schoolhouse closed.

Sometimes, educators ruminate about one-room
schoolhouses. They point to closer teacher-student rela-
tionships, to the freer hand of teachers, to the presence of
more mature role models for younger children as all being
reflective of a more effective, personalized form of education. Some of these attributes might be ascribed to education along the Fremont but, with the spectacles of
nostalgia removed, the reviewer's eye looks back over a
very mixed blessing of learning and growing—and sometimes chaos.

Most teachers who taught in Fruita from 1900 until
1941 were young women recently graduated from their
teacher training. It is doubtful whether any were over-
joyed at the thought of living in the sometimes stupefying
isolation. One retired teacher described the dismay she
felt on being assigned to so remote and uncivilized a
place, although she thought Fruita "beautiful." As late as
1934, she had available only "a few old, ragged books."
Along the river, a young teacher's social life would be
extremely limited and the immediate support and guid-
ance of more experienced teachers or principal lacking.
Most stayed a year, got some qualifying experience, and
moved on to more civilized parts. A teacher usually

A Receding Sea of Faces . . .

As the years rolled by, classes at the schoolhouse grew steadily smaller. Ida May Stevenson (top) had at least twenty-two students in 1912, while Julia Mott Hickman (middle) taught only fourteen in 1925. By 1935, teacher Janice Oldroyd's class (bottom) comprised only nine students. The school closed in 1941.

1912

1925

1935

boarded with a local family. One reported trouble with seemingly omnipresent bed bugs. A student told her not to mind, saying "everybody's got 'em."

In more civilized rural areas of Utah, the Mormon Church exercised a firm control over human moral behavior, both by heavy peer pressure and by the commanding watchfulness of self-assured Church leaders. This influence seemed markedly weaker the farther one journeyed into the hinterlands, perhaps because these isolated areas attracted many mavericks and bred a rough-and-tumble progeny who resisted conformity and discipline.

Pity the young teacher arriving in any of the river settlements—not necessarily Fruita—to take up her new post! From the start, her will and courage would be put to sometimes brutal testing by a few students. If she survived without being cowed or falling to pieces, she would probably last the entire school year and be the catalyst for some genuine learning. Some teachers proved to be as tough as rawhide, but a few could not take the teasing, bullying, and rowdiness and were literally driven out of town. It must have been a crushing experience for the teacher and reflected no credit on the parents of the tormentors.

Fruita students saw quite a mixture in teacher quality. One former student described a teacher who chewed gum all the time, simply sat at her desk, made the children read their few cast-off books constantly, and did no instructing whatsoever. This student was determined to chew gum to spite her, which resulted in a comically-described wrestling match on the floor with her trying to pry the gum from his mouth. She was bitten on the hand for her efforts and the student was expelled for two weeks. However, enough of the Fruita teachers are respectfully and fondly remembered to restore a measure of faith in the strength of human character. A few went on to long and distinguished careers in education.

The schoolhouse became *the* public building in Fruita and was long used as a church meeting house and social hall as well as a school. The desks were not attached to the floor so they could be moved to make dancing possible, even though Fruita was not as fortunate in the

fiddler department as was, for example, Blue Valley, where all the Hunt family were skilled players.

Fruita residents never did get their own church building, but they did receive authorization for a post office about 1904. They were forced to change the name of the community from Junction to an apt Fruita to be approved by the Post Office Department; there were too many towns named Junction in Utah.

The photographer caught the interior of the Fruita schoolhouse just prior to its closing in 1941. Teachers often altered the spartan furnishing arrangement.

Joseph Ridley Cook and Mary Ann Taylor Cook were married in 1879 and moved to Fruita around the turn of the century. Like so many couples in late frontier Utah, they moved frequently and had huge families. As chronicled by son James (see photo opposite), his parents lived in St. George, Thurber (now Bicknell), Washington, Vernal, Teasdale, Price, and Fruita. They had fifteen children, three of whom—Barbara Ellen, Joseph, and David Allen—died within a week of one another in Bicknell during a devastating diphtheria epidemic in 1890. Baby Willie was born in Fruita and died there, apparently, in 1901.

It is very difficult for the historian to get close to the pioneer residents of Fruita before or near the turn of the century; no journals or diaries have been found and all of the early settlers were long dead when this writer began to interview former residents. Because of this, the few existing recollections about them as human beings are especially precious.

Earlier, we noted Mrs. Evangeline Godby's visit with the Cooks in Fruita in 1908. She came up from Caineville over the Blue Dugway and recalled the jarring wagon ride down Danish Hill (near the Fruita campground). She was only five:

> *I remember we came down over the Danish Hill and my brother riding along beside the wagon. Mother and Father were coming up to see Aunt Mary Ann and Uncle Joe. They were coming to Fruita to have my sister Laura named. My father was known for never starting to go anywhere before it was too late to get there in daylight. We were always late. I remember being very small and wandering around the yard there at my aunt's place and that they were all in bed already. I went over to the door of the house.*

Apparently young Evangeline woke her Uncle Joe, who tried to awake his wife, Mary Ann. Mrs Godby went on:

> *Uncle Joe called "Mary Ann, Mary Ann, get up!" Mary Ann said, "I took native herb pills (laxatives) last night and I wouldn't get up for my grandmother." When she got*

Alexander Abendego "Abbie" Clarke and Martha Catherine "Katy" Clarke were contemporaries of the Cooks who stayed in Fruita about a decade. Four of their fourteen children—some of which are shown here at the left—were born in Fruita.

up the next morning she was the happiest woman alive. Oh, Aunt Mary Ann—I just loved the next morning— she fed us fried cheese and everything. It was the most delightful breakfast!

I remember Grandfather David Cook, who was blind. He was a very handsome old man with delicate features and a long, white beard. Mother put Laura on a chair, and grandfather knelt beside it to name her.

It was a tender moment for all then and reveals to the modern outsider something about the closeness of Mormon families.

ABOVE: James Cook

RIGHT: James Cook's first wife, Rebecca, was photographed in Fruita shortly before the couple's failed attempt at a homestead in rugged Blue Valley, further down the Fremont River.

Brigham Young, the farsighted President of the Church of Jesus Christ of Latter-day Saints was revered by the Mormons as their "prophet, seer, and revelator" but often vilified by others. The anti-Mormon writer of *Conquering the West*, "Colonel" Frank Triplett, raged obscurely in 1883 that "... we find in him a mixture of Mokanna, the veiled prophet of Kohrassan, and that terrible chief of the assassins, the Old Man of the Mountain." Their practice of plural marriage before 1890 stirred up deep hostility toward the Mormon people and resulted in the Edmunds Laws, which made polygamy a federal crime. Brigham Young's iron will, determination and influence on western history are legendary.

Fruita had no church house and has been described by one local old timer as "only a ranch town." A community without a church building and its own Mormon bishop (equivalent in function to a parish priest or minister) seems to have had little status in Mormon country's backwaters. Further down the river, Caineville, Blue Valley, and Hanksville all had bishops and church buildings. What about religious life in Fruita?

In the early days, all Fruita residents were—at least in name—Mormons. Most had been raised in the Church but some had drifted away from regular worship and obedience to moral strictures and teachings; these were "Jack Mormons."

Those close to the church regularly attended Sunday school, which is a persons-of-all-ages institution for the Saints. Turn-of-the-century Torrey Bishop John Riley Stewart wrote fondly of visits with the Saints of Fruita to hold Sacrament meetings (holy communion). He spoke especially well of Amasa Pierce who, as presiding elder at Fruita, reported directly to Bishop Stewart. Sacrament meetings were held in Fruita homes, as well as in the school. Not too oddly, Bishop Stewart's pastoral visits to Fruita always seemed to increase during the fruit harvest season.

Bishop Stewart recorded the following on Sunday, December 15, 1901:

> *Attended Sunday school and had a very nice time. Gathered up statistical reports of the branch during noon hour and took dinner with Abbie Clark. Had a lovely meeting, a very goodly spirit present. Went to teacher meeting at Sister Leo Holt's [Rena Holt], it being different from any I ever attended. All would meet at a certain house and they would hold a regular meeting, each one speaking. It pleased me very much as I liked that way of teaching the people. Stayed at Brother Pierce's.*

Mormons are not known for deviating spontaneously from traditional methods in religious education. Could this innovation indicate something about a greater independence of mind among the Saints along the Fremont?

Bishop John Riley Stewart of Torrey saw to the needs of the Latter-day Saints faithful in Fruita at the turn of the century.

In looking back at the early days of the century, one sees an out-of-focus picture of the moral influence of religion in Fruita and the Fremont River towns in general. Even among the Saints who participated in church life, heavy drinking by some seems to have been a problem—no doubt to alleviate the unending boredom of heavy toil and isolation. Social drinking had been forbidden by the Mormon Word of Wisdom, a requirement widely ignored along a river where moonshining had become a way of life. A Jack Mormon in a turn-of-the-century, strait-laced town in Rabbit Valley could not have long borne the ostracism that would have been forthcoming for openly "carrying on." Even today, one detects a bit of disdain on the part of some "up county" natives for those "down county" and it probably stems from those frontier times when people along the river seemed rougher. The river towns were "south of the border" to other county residents.

What might have been seen by some as a morally lax environment was, however, fairly staid when compared to better-known frontier communities of an earlier day in Dodge City, Kansas, or Tombstone, Arizona. Colorful though it may have been, the story of the Fremont River settlements was painted in far more subdued shades than either of those places.

If life in the valley of the Fremont *was* gentler—if no less difficult—than many backwaters of the frontier outside of Utah, then no small credit for this goes to faithful, practicing Mormon men and women. In every river settlement, devout Saints added a strong-willed, kindly leaven to a robust frontiersman mix. In times of sickness, death, or misadventure, it was not only the Bishop's storehouse that was opened to the hurt or destitute, but the hearts of Latter-day Saints who seemed convinced—as was the hymnwriter—that "Our God will never us forsake."

New orchards in Fruita flourished as General "Black Jack" Pershing was landing in Europe with his American Expeditionary Force in 1917.

We'll find the place,
which God for us prepared

W hat was it like to live in isolated Fruita before it was discovered by the National Park Service? To find some of the answers, we need to visit an earlier twentieth century Fruita through the eyes of one-time residents.

Not surprisingly, views differ. One relative latecomer, G. Dewey Gifford, had very pleasant memories of his more than forty-year residency and referred to Fruita as a "paradise." On the other hand, G. Neldon Adams, who came to Fruita as a boy in 1914 and whose family left just before Gifford's arrival in 1927, had vivid memories, too, but was glad to leave. He remembered Fruita as "poverty flats."

No doubt much of the disparity in these recollections can be explained by the fact that Neldon Adams was a teenager here, kind of an involuntary, hard-working prisoner in a social isolation that he yearned to transcend. Dewey Gifford, on the other hand, came here as a newly-married, resolute, and self-sufficient man who was seeking to make a home and prosper in a landscape he found beautiful and challenging. The differences in their perceptions, perhaps explicable, are still interesting.

OPPOSITE: Fruita as Dewey Gifford knew it. Fruita was still living close to its frontier origins in 1931 when this photograph was taken from the escarpment. In those days, the road to Hanksville twisted along the west face of Capitol Reef and through Capitol Gorge. Within a decade after this photograph was taken, the creation of Capitol Reef National Monument would initiate fundamental changes in community life and character.

Most of the Andrew Adams family was caught by this circa 1919 snapshot. In front, left to right, stand Clifford and Dee. In the second row are Novella and Orville, and in the third row stand Neldon and his mother, Harriet.

Father Andrew Adams displays what the 1918 photographer recorded as a "watermelon-eating grin."

POVERTY FLATS

Neldon Adams' father bought old Joe Cook's twenty-odd acres in 1914. By then, some of the land had changed hands from the first homesteaders and their neighbors were M. Valentine (Tine) Oyler, Calvin Pendleton, "Will" Behunin, Clyde Behunin, the Blackburns, the Chesnuts, the Carrells and the Motts. While Neldon was there, Clarence Mulford and Jorgan Jorgenson bought out "Cal" Pendleton, and young Merin Smith arrived to eventually marry one of the Oyler girls and take up farming.

The Adams family was large—not unusual for Utah Mormons—and consisted of mother Harriet; brothers Myrtus, Farrell, Orville, Clifford, and Dee; and sisters Reeda, Novella, Fauntella, and Hazel.

Neldon's father, Andrew, worked away often as a sheepherder to earn the cash that was otherwise nonexistent in a part of America where bartering was status quo (and is still widespread). Much tedious farm work fell to young Neldon on the twenty-acre farm that was about half orchards and half pasture and hayfields. One job he particularly despised was the frequent and backbreaking cleaning of irrigation ditches that rapidly silted in, especially the ditches from aptly-named Sand (Sulphur) Creek. It was the massive silting-in of such ditches by floods in Caineville that broke the spirits—as well as the backs—of some of the toughest human beings on the American frontier.

LEFT: Youngsters Dee (left) and Clifford Adams pose on the running board of a Model T Ford.

BELOW LEFT: Hazel Adams, as a young woman, stands near a fence by the M. Valentine Oyler place about 1920.

BELOW: Novella Adams holds baby Dee in the front yard of their Fruita home. As poor as they were, father Andrew took time for amenities like a picket fence. Some kind of a front yard fence was needed to keep then-huge trailing livestock herds away from the house and vegetable gardens.

The Oyler family was especially well remembered by Neldon Adams. Sisters Clara, Cora, and Carrie sit atop "Johnnie" (held by father Michael Valentine Oyler) about 1915.

The Mining Bust

As early as 1893, the gently rising landform to the west of today's Scenic Drive was intensively explored by prospectors looking for gold, silver, copper and lead. They found nothing worth mining and their only legacy is the name of the landform—Miners Mountain.

Closer to Fruita, the west end of Grand Wash caught the attention of prospectors just after the turn of the century. The first claimants were after gold, silver and copper in the Shinarump formation, but in 1904 Thomas Nixon and J. C. Sumner (perhaps Jack Sumner, the second in command of Major Powell's 1869 Colorado River expedition) filed a uranium claim. Nixon dug a tunnel of one hundred feet and started a second; he also began building a stone house on the claim. Soon after 1911, the claim seems to have been abandoned. Uranium was thought to have valuable medicinal properties, both when taken internally and packed in pouches worn on the outside of the body.

On October 1, 1935, a consortium of individuals filed on the old Nixon Claim. One of these was Michael Valentine Oyler of Fruita and his name somehow became attached to the mine. The story of the Oyler Mine in the 1940s and 1950s is a fascinating one but outside the scope of this book.

Neldon remembers that he was doing "a man's work" when he wasn't big enough "to reach the trips on the hayrake" (a horse-drawn machine that gathered cut hay in rows). Besides school, he milked a few cows every day, cut wood, hauled water barrels up from the creek and—in season—picked fruit. He helped his father haul the fruit up the valley in their Studebaker wagon to sell or barter for grain and cheese.

Neldon was often bored and got into more than a little mischief. One spring, all the cats in Fruita seemed to come down with a mysterious affliction that resulted in their tails falling off—"bobtailing"—or so it was first thought around town. It wasn't until Neldon's co-conspirator—Jessie Richardson—broke a vow of silence that the people in Fruita found out that he and Jessie had been chopping off the poor felines' tails with a hatchet. Neldon fondly remembers his mother's declaration that "if it wasn't so cussfired funny, I'd skin you alive." He was the recalcitrant schoolhouse gum chewer we mentioned earlier, and he once climbed to the roof of the schoolhouse when the stove was fired up and threw black pepper down the chimney, causing convulsive sneezes.

As he matured, Neldon's thoughts turned to girls; there were a few nearly his age around Fruita. He especially remembered "Tine" Oyler's attractive daughters Cora and Carrie. The sudden, tragic death of beautiful Carrie, hospitalized for appendicitis, stunned the community and was a hard blow for her family.

Teenagers often swam in a Fremont River hole in back of the still-standing Gifford house. They often held

48

Most of the Fruita Oylers stand before the cliffs of the escarpment near the site of the present Highway 24 petroglyph parking area about 1928. From left to right are Elvera Oyler, Michael Valentine Oyler, Dee Richardson, unknown, Merin Smith and Cora Oyler Smith. By then, Cora was the only one of Elvera Oyler's daughters that was still alive; she lived in Fruita for almost fifty years.

dances and enjoyed candy pulls and chicken roasts. The boys were responsible for catching and killing the chickens, the girls for roasting them. Neldon reports the adventure of a foray up the valley to obtain chickens; once he and two pals liberated some from captivity, and they really had a feast. There wasn't much in the way of music for these parties—just a harmonica or a poor fiddle—although the Oylers had a player piano and the Adams family owned an Edison cylinder phonograph. Even into the mid-1920s, no one had yet acquired a battery radio.

Apparently, the first motor vehicle owned by a Fruita resident was this General Motors Corporation "Model 15" truck. It was purchased by partners Cliff Barton and Tine Oyler from the Randall-Dodd Auto Company in Salt Lake City in 1917.

Myrtus Adams was especially fond of Carrie Oyler, the Oyler's eldest daughter, seen here at about age sixteen. In those days, the high school-age children of Fruita residents were required to board up the valley during the school year. While living in Bicknell, she suffered a burst appendix and although operated on in Richfield, died a week later. The "good old days" before antibiotics were not good days for Carrie.

Going up in the valley was something you could look forward to, remembered Neldon, "you could even buy a candy bar" from Bishop Pectol's general store in Torrey. Neldon, who was always small, liked to attend the big dances there, but had to make his mark with his fists until the local boys no longer tested him.

Neldon knew well and worked for all the farmer-moonshiners around Fruita. The hardest work in making moonshine was the hauling of large quantities of water to dry, cliffside hideaways, although one site—Whiskey Springs—was well supplied. Liquor distillers made some potent shine from corn mash, fruit, and sometimes exotica like "the green skimmings of molasses" when nothing else was available. They also put up enormous quantities of grape wine. All this brought in cash revenues from thirsty sheepherders, cattlemen and others. Legend has it that hard-drinking, traveling sheepshearers consumed by far the greatest quantities of these products. Much moonshine was consumed right there in Fruita, too, according to Neldon.

The valley of the Fremont was so remote that the great care taken to conceal stills and liquor caches was mostly unnecessary. It appears that moonshiners had little to fear from local law enforcement officers. Once, however, their care in concealment paid off. Automobiles were a rare occurrence in Fruita and when one arrived at 2:30 A.M. one morning in 1918 everyone was alerted. It was a huge touring car full of determined state revenue agents. The next day, the "revenuers" found a big cache of the most widely known of the Fruita moonshiners (hidden under the hinged deck of a front porch) but they failed to ferret out the producing stills. It caused quite a stir, but the local moonshiners' operations were rarely bothered again.

Life in and around Fruita was sometimes physically violent, according to Neldon, who often proved he could handle himself. Neldon remembered young Merin Smith, Tine Oyler's hired man, as a nice fellow but no one to be

trifled with. Also, heavy-drinking, camping cattlemen liked to fight, especially when "well-oiled," as Neldon put it. Nearby town dances—mostly sponsored by the Mormon Church—very often included a big brawl as a sideshow, unscheduled of course. But the rough stuff was not the deadly kind, at least most of the time.

Neldon remembered one time when a local farmer was insulted by a cowboy during a camp house drinking spree and took off after his rifle. Fortunately for all, the farmer passed out in the creek on the way back from his home. One time Neldon personally witnessed a gunfight over the whereabouts of a woman that left one man wounded. The wounded man was able to drive away in his Model T Ford, however.

People passing through Fruita were always of interest. Besides sheepherders, cattlemen, and sheepshearers, Neldon reported a few strange travelers, especially gypsies. Neldon recalled an incident when an old gypsy woman offered to read his fortune if he would gather a pile of firewood. He did so, but she refused to pay off. When he threatened to tell his father and complained bitterly to the gypsy leader, she told his fortune in detail—really "laid it on thick," according to Neldon.

Fruita was rarely a stop for dignitaries but Governor Dern of Utah stopped long enough to pose with Julia Mott Hickman's class from the Fruita school in 1925.

The old Oyler place stood where Highway 24 passes the petroglyph parking area, just over one mile east of the visitor center. The girl is Cora Oyler Smith, about 1917.

Gypsies in Utah?

As hard as it may be to believe, it appears that authentic, itinerant Gypsies added color and excitement to life in remote Mormon Utah villages like Fruita at the turn of the century. A historian records:

It is not known exactly when the Gypsies first came to Utah, and accounts regarding the frequency of their visits also vary. Kate Snow states that, "Rare were the occasions when an adventuresome band would brave the rough, dusty road in quest of a little easy money." However, others report that Gypsies were regular visitors in the early 1900s to small Utah communities during the spring and summer months.

In Elsinore, Utah, the Gypsies were known to visit the community every year during the summer and stay for about a month. Myrtle Western, a resident of Deseret for over sixty years, remembered when the Gypsies made their annual trips to that area. She did not remember the same groups coming back. It was always a different group who would come. However, Lavern Rigby Johnson stated, "In the early 1900s, many gypsies traveled Echo Canyon during the seasons that roads were passable. They were always traveling west. The same gypsies called at the ranches so frequently that they were known by name and their individual personality quirks were learned."

Who were these nomadic people who made their appearance in rural Utah communities? Historians generally agree that they were of Hindu origin and were primarily from northern India. Some believe they left India around A.D. 100. Others believe they were exiled because of their religious beliefs or ran away from the persecution of Tamerlane or Timur, the great Tartar conqueror who invaded India in 1398.

The Gypsies brought excitement and adventure to remote farming communities. Myrtle Western recounted, "We always knew when the Gypsies were in town. As soon as the kids saw them they would call out, 'The Gypsies are coming, the Gypsies are coming.' Kids further down the street would pick up on the call and relay it on down the street until everyone knew the Gypsies were in town."

Lucile Roper Hales, a life-long resident of the Pahvant Valley, explained, "We had a big brass bucket and a small one. The Gypsies tried to get them from us one time to make jewelry. After that, as soon as we found out that the Gypsies were in town we would run home as fast as we could, calling, 'Mama, hide the brass buckets, the Gypsies are coming!"

Exotic visitors always attracted attention. Kate Snow noted, "... the men with their big hats and spangled vests, the women with their full skirts, figured waists, braids of black hair and large earrings. ... They would always have, besides the wagons, horses, dogs and children, some added attraction. One band that came to Manti had a large black bear that would dance. He wore a muzzle to which a chain was attached. The trainer held the chain and directed the dance. They also had an organ grinder and a monkey that never missed catching the nickels that were thrown to him. The whole population turned out to see the strange people, and enjoy their entertainment. No advertising was necessary—by word of mouth the whole population soon knew of the attraction."

—from "The Gypsies are Coming!" by David A. Hales in the *Utah Historical Quarterly*, Fall, 1985.

When he was quite young, Neldon's forthrightness almost earned him a swift kick from a traveler. Two men in a big Pierce Arrow touring car came through wearing dusters, goggles, and gloves—early sightseers. Pointing up the road to Capitol Gorge they asked about the mileage in the peculiar Utah idiom of the day, "How do you call it to Hanksville?' Neldon, taking them literally, responded with the only name he had ever heard *for* the road and declared loudly "a rough sonofabitch!" Neldon recalled that they chased him into the house without catching him, but they offered to apply one of their black leather boots to his posterior.

The orchards of Fruita had become very productive by the First World War. Sheltered by the red rock walls of the Fremont River Canyon and well watered, new orchards like those of Michael Valentine Oyler, seen at left, prospered. Few suspected that "Tine," the conservative older man that they knew in the 1930s, had dabbled in more radical politics as a young man. For about six months in 1908, Tine had been a paid-up member of the Socialist Party of America, called by one writer "hornets in the beehive of Zion."

Dewey Gifford's children attended the one-room school. Brothers Lloyd and Fay are seated at the very center of this circa 1935 photograph, taken just behind the school building.

PARADISE

Dewey Gifford was a tall, powerfully-built, quiet man who was, for much of his life, a devout practicing Mormon. He and his wife, Nell, bought out her dad (Jorgan Jorgenson) and went on to raise a family of four children—Lloyd, Fay, Dale, and Twila—in a two-story, stucco house near the Fremont River. If any man made a reasonable success of living and farming in Fruita it was "Dew" Gifford. In 1927 his neighbors were William Chesnut, a widower with four children; Al Chesnut; Merin and Cora (Oyler) Smith; Guy Smith; Clarence "Cass" Mulford; Dan Adams; and Tine Oyler.

Dewey had worked in the Wyoming oil fields to earn a stake but he was—soul and sinew—a farmer. He was known as a tireless and thrifty worker, but he had to learn the fruit business mostly by listening to some good advice and by trial and error. On occasion, experience was a pitiless teacher and Dewey remembered losing a whole grove of apricot trees, because he gave them too much water from his irrigation ditches. To bring in cash, he "worked state road" part time for several years.

As far as farming was concerned, the fruit trees were everything. Except for vegetable gardens, the only other crop was hay for the animals, although some sorghum

Gifford Homestead

In 1996 the Capitol Reef Natural History Association, in cooperation with the National Park Service, renovated and refurbished the Gifford farmhouse as a cultural demonstration site to interpret the early Mormon settlement of the Fruita valley. The house depicts the typical spartan nature of rural Utah farm homes of the early 1900s. In addition to the farmhouse, the Gifford homestead includes a barn, smokehouse, garden, pasture, and rock walls.

The Gifford Homestead is located one mile south of the visitor center on the Scenic Drive. Parking is available at the picnic area. The home is open seasonally.

Early visitors to Capitol Reef National Monument found the unpaved roads difficult in wet weather. Here, Dewey Gifford provides assistance with his tractor about 1945.

The Gifford's neighbors in Fruita, just to the north, were Merin and Cora Oyler Smith. Merin Smith, who owned a "real hot" V8 Ford in the early 1930s, is shown here, with son Ed.

had been grown earlier in the century. Horse-drawn equipment was primitive, even for Depression America, with walking plows, heavy wagons, dump rakes, and mowing machines mostly in evidence. Dewey borrowed a sulky plow from Torrey from time to time. All these implements were pulled not by classic draft horse breeds, but by multi-purpose animals used for both saddle and harness—"plugs," Neldon called them. In Dewey's younger days, Fruita residents were acquiring cars and trucks; young Merin Smith had the hottest machine in Fruita, an early V-8 Ford.

It wasn't until the eve of World War II that the first tractor was purchased by a Fruita resident. It was a strange, attention-getting machine called a "Power Horse," made in Salt Lake City by the Eimco Corporation and purchased by Merin Smith. Mating an Allis-Chalmers "B" engine to an Eimco-designed, four-wheel drive chassis, the Power Horse steering levers were controlled by reins from the seat of the trailing hay rake, mowing machine, harrow, or the like. It could turn on a dime and just as readily turn over in a ditch. The Eimco Corporation creation was supposed to convince backwater farmers still using flesh-and-blood horses that they could easily switch to a Power Horse without having to discard their old-horse-era farm implements. Some were convinced, but not enough, and only a few Power Horses were ever built.

By Dewey's day, Mormons were journeying to Torrey for worship and other activities. In 1900, it had taken two hours by buggy over the steep, twisting dirt road; by 1930, a car or pickup could climb the grade in a half hour. It seems that only a few adult males in Fruita were practicing elders in the Church in 1930 and this appears to have been a significant decline from the turn-of-the-century period. In 1930, Fruita stood outside the mainstream of Wayne County in more ways than geography.

Spring and summer were busy times—first pruning and hauling off cuttings, then irrigating and fruit picking. Women "bottled" foods at a furious pace in the summer to get ready for winter. Fall was a time to slaughter hogs, sometimes a steer, and to salt down meat for the winter. Dew Gifford was one of a few Fruita residents to smoke pork as well as salt it; he inherited a good smokehouse from his father-in-law and used it often. He favored not the abundant applewood of Fruita for smoking, but green cottonwood instead.

In the dead of winter, Nell Gifford sewed most of the family's clothes, except for the overalls worn by men and boys. She quilted, mostly with her two half-sisters in Fruita, Dicey Chesnut and Marie Mulford. Besides mending fences and tending to the equipment, winter was a time of boredom and bouts of cabin fever. People passed around well-read books, played cards, listened to the battery radio and usually went to bed early.

Family outings were much anticipated. It was easy to catch huge trout not too far up the Fremont canyon, and high country deer hunting expeditions were a major source of pleasure (by 1930, not a deer was to be found near Fruita; they had long been hunted out). Occasionally, trips were made to Richfield and Salina, although the

Another Gifford neighbor, Dan Adams, poses above.

From left to right Dan Adams with his children, Vie, Dan, and Marcia photographed about 1912.

For many years, Dewey Gifford's neighbor just to the south was fruit grower and rancher Clarence "Cass" Mulford. Mulford's wife, Marie, was a half-sister to Dewey's wife, Nell.

OPPOSITE: This photograph was taken from Cass Mulford's property and captures some of the contrasts and charm of an agrarian scene in one of America's prime scenic resources.

road was unpaved almost the entire distance—about eighty miles. In Fruita, holidays were marked by picnics and baseball games on homemade diamonds.

Dewey became and remained an ardent Franklin D. Roosevelt democrat, pretty rare in conservative rural Utah. He and republican neighbor Cass Mulford often had some spirited political discussions.

Dewey's sons went off to war in the early 1940s, surviving service with the U.S. Navy. Dewey continued to do well in Fruita because he never ceased working. As visitors started arriving to see Capitol Reef National Monument he saw new opportunity; Dewey tore down the decrepit camp house and replaced it with a small motel, becoming an innkeeper as well as a farmer. Dewey even took a job with the maintenance force of the park, but in his late sixties he took the cash offered by the government for his farm and he and Nell moved to comfortable new quarters in Torrey, very close to the little church they loved. They were the last of the old timers to leave, and they closed the book on a little-known but fascinating chapter in Utah history.

All is well, all is well

The inclusion of Fruita within the boundaries of a new national monument in 1937 resulted in major impacts on a little hamlet almost lost in frontier times. The new monument was the result of the hard work of two local men—Joseph Hickman and Ephraim Pectol—but that is another story.

As word spread slowly in the 1930s about the scenic beauty of the Capitol Reef area (a particularly striking section of the Waterpocket Fold between the Fremont River and Pleasant Creek), adventurous outsider sightseers began to trickle into Fruita. Some, like historian-writer Charles Kelly and a dentist-turned-rockhound, Arthur (Doc) Inglesby, fell in love with the Fremont River Valley. Inglesby bought land from a farmer and was soon followed by others, like cartoonist Richard Sprang (Batman comics), and Dean Brimhall, retired from the U.S. Department of Commerce and an amateur explorer. A new breed of settlers had arrived in Fruita, not farmers this time, but red rock desert lovers.

Historian Charles Kelly (author of *The Outlaw Trail*) became the new monument's unpaid custodian in the early 1940s and later its first ranger and superintendent. The years of Kelly's dedicated administration

Pictured in the building adjacent to the Pectol store in Torrey are Ephraim Porter Pectol, his wife Dorothy Hickman Pectol, and Della Taylor Hickman, wife of Joseph Smith Hickman. Ephraim Porter Pectol and Joseph Smith Hickman were instrumental in the preservation of what is now Capitol Reef National Park.

Charles Kelly, historian and prolific writer, was Capitol Reef's first ranger and, later, superintendent. He was committed to preservation and deeply resented the opening of the monument to uranium prospecting during the 1950s.

comprise another entrancing tale. As colorful characters go—and Utah's parks had many in the early days—Kelly stood in a class by himself.

As monument visitation increased in the 1950s, many of the old-time Fruita residents turned to serving visitor needs as a supplement to their incomes. Essentially, a frontier way of life—extremely isolated and closed to outside influences—was gone forever. In the late 1950s, the National Park Service began to purchase private property in Fruita. By the time that Capitol Reef National Park was created in 1971 virtually all the former farmlands of Fruita were in federal ownership.

Today, the National Park Service has come to view the Fruita saga as having importance in telling the bigger story of a diverse, rural America. Two themes—Utah's role in the closing of the frontier and life in an isolated, rural America dominated by one religious persuasion—have rare interpretive value. Fruita is now administered as a cultural landscape, marked by thousands of fruit trees and enriched by remnant historic buildings. At Capitol Reef National Park, visitors find that cultural and natural resources can reinforce and enhance one another to everyone's greater reward. For many, Fruita becomes a cultural portal to a fuller appreciation of the natural world.

Few outsiders came to know the isolated communities of south-central Utah better than writer Wallace

Arthur "Doc" Inglesby, a retired dentist and avid rockhound, was one of the desert lovers who found Fruita in the late 1930s, along with others like Charles Kelly, Richard Sprang, Dean Brimhall, and Max Krueger.

Stegner, whose *Mormon Country* has become a classic and whose gentle words about Fruita grace the beginning of this book. Maybe it betrays the history lover in me and puts me at odds with the classic naturalists, but I nod an affirming assent when Stegner declares in *American Places:* "The land is not complete without its human history and associations."

Some of us might add, "its ghosts, too."

Photographs of the homes of Fruita pioneers and early residents are scarce. Many homes were log cabins or houses of simple board-and-batten construction. Dicey Ann Chesnut, half-sister of Nell Gifford, lived in this simple structure for many years and was well-known to travelers as a hospitable and generous woman. She is fondly remembered by many in Wayne County, and it was the way of life that she personified that was so vividly etched in the memory of historian Wallace Stegner.